Set the Night Singing

TRICIA D. WAGNER

LYRIDAE BOOKS

*To the characters
peopling my story worlds –
you are my muse.*

*Without you
I'd be lost.*

One

I close my eyes upon the night,
 and there to my delight I see –
 not dark of self,
 nor quiet void,
 but specters from my story shelf.

In light of day, they walk as shades
 in other realms, yet by my side.
 In deeps of darkness, though,
 they near –
 my lonely room grows occupied.

Lounging 'gainst the headboard, leaning in,
 whispering their secrets and their pain,
 in deepest confidence we speak 'till dawn,
 when with my ink, I render them again.

Two

The
silent
twilight rings
with golden sunbeams
with cicada song.
Alone with you −
ecstasy.
Come, stars.
Rise.

Three

Between two boards
    sleeps paper pressed
    plain black and white
    though not at rest.

For when the pages
    my eyes meet −
    a rush of wings
    of running feet,
    of starships launched,
    a conquest dire,
    a maiden fighting
    dragon fire.

A double spell
    make mind and page,
    in concord fly
    their broken cage.

Four

Beauty to shock to life
    to stop mid-sentence
    to drop dead –
    moth of the moon
    in cloak of sea foam
    black rimmed as a bight
    as the belly of a crescented star
    a creature with tails and with eyespots,
    antennae of angel wings curled.

How can you be so scarce
    how can I fail to see, to search
    that my eyes might delight
    in this gift –
    but you're gone.
    And so is the light of the spring night
    drawn over my sight like a cloak.

Where you fly,
    one so bright
    so not of Earth
    so of the Earth –
    flicker your candle, I'll follow –
    I'm lost.

Five

Hope, ever the huntsman,
    knows well these wilds.

"Where go we?" I plead.
    Walking on, he keeps silent,
    his quiet quieting me.

Through thickets, though storms rage
    I – seeing
    follow

as he,
    child of forests,
    most clever
    stalks on.

Six

Starlight glimmers on the waves,
    a strike of foresight, mere a flash
    of whispers from the sunken caves,
    from ships long-moored and heroes brash.

The Earth's expanse
    keeps mighty deeds –

so set the sails
    to twilight's gold –

and cut the anchor,
    dare the deeps,

and from bleak storms
    remake the bold –

brave champions
    and their histories.

Seven

A last mark laid upon the page –
    I rise – the masterpiece complete!

A voice of love from deep within:
    "You're not near finished. Take a seat."

I sight a character, in gist –
    a flash of face and echoing feet.

So pleased I rise! Until I'm pressed:
    "You know him little. Take your seat."

THE END I pen. With joy, I rise!
    My book – a burning star – casts heat.

The muse of artistry stands by –
    "A good beginning. Take your seat."

Eight

When fall I restless or fast into sorrow
    when air is as water to breathe
    when light burns
    and the shadows devour my spark –

slip I to the wilds
    where the wildest of all –
    oak elder, ash arcing, and aspen soft call.

My fingertips handling course tree skin
    the smell of the sap running deep
    the pull of the roots
    and the broad rings of trunk
    and ozonic breath cooling me –

I am staid. I find industry.
    Satedness. Peace.

For a tree great grandfather
    to me bending low,
    limb hands supporting his vast weight –
    he lends all his strength.

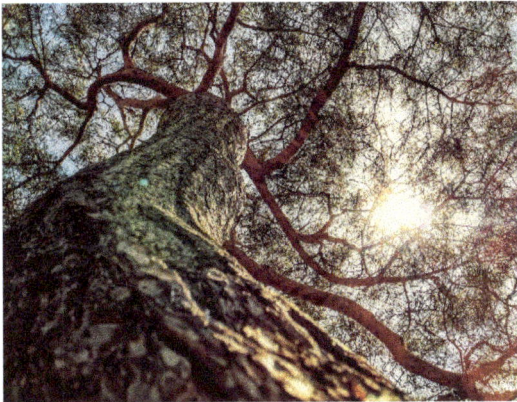

Nine

The wind will break limbs.
    Lightning might breech stone.
    In time, break shall all.

Wisdom wails not at the storm
    but lantern in hand ushers us deeper in.

Ingenuity rages not at the strike
    but seeks science to channel its strength.

The muse weeps not at the breaking
    but walks alongside,
    whispering questions.

Ten

An animated spirit lives
 within this carapace of bone.
 The spirit, though, not bounded be
 but draws the air of spaces free.

For while one body is her lot –
 her train of footprints shows one set –
 the spirit plays at marionettes
 walking joints down parapets.

Seeing skin, don't by mistake
 conclude the mind you comprehend.
 The true home that she occupies
 is bounded by the starry skies.

And spirits all, too vast for Earth,
 toe-touching waters, grazing sod,
 want starfields worn as cloaks and gowns,
 and galaxies to don for crowns.

Eleven

Words unsaid,
    blank – the mind
    narrows.

Words on tongue
    or in the heart –
    mountains.

Words artisted,
    crafted fine –
    arrows.

Words let loose
    from aquifers –
    fountains.

Twelve

The lion weeping, thorn in paw,
   the dove with broken wings,
   the splinter in the child's hand –
   these are no trifling things.

I thank the doctor first who said,
   "I know a better way."
   Who put the needle back to bed
   and gently saved the day.

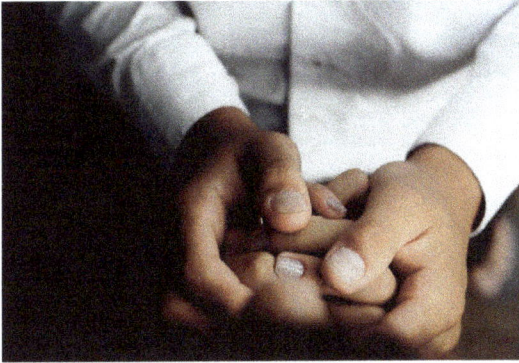

Thirteen

In cavern's damp, inside discoverer's
    lamplight, kneel

full patient for Earth's spirit to arrive and sit
    at potter's wheel

and spin creations slick of mineral made
    by rainstorm leavings.

Enough is here in magic stones that jewels
    fire flashing grow.

So bear I pen in hand, in stillness listen
    as the music swells.

Fourteen

The chasm laid twixt life and death –
    unbreachable from either side.

Yet letters, syllables, and words –
    such simple things,
    yet born with wings.

Thus sing the living to the passed,
    and catch the thoughts the ancients cast.

Fifteen

I stepped into the forest
    peace to find
    but rather found
    a village all abustle
    with a song
    of summer sounds.

So dove I in with naught to lose
    but time
    and this the forest chorus
    chased full fast
    and kept me wandering
    present

by the tall grass
    hoppers winging
    by the stream
    its bullfrog singing
    by the stretching legs
    of pine
    by nectar cups
    upheld on blooms
    to buzzing bees

and so receive I
    forest wisdom
    and depart the revel
    full of songs –
    words my pen
    can play again
    when need I peace
    to right the wrongs.

Sixteen

Give me letters to spin – twenty-six.
    This is how two people square.

The teaching hands point
    when the words are too straight.
    Every character needs love,
    even those who oppose.

I blaze
    as the wisdom sinks deep –

to these worlds I've created,
    my teacher has ventured with me.

Seventeen

If academics prisons be,
    for sake of gods, imprison me.

I fear no form, no history,
    but quake and shake at entropy.

This head is heavy, not for sleep,
    but for the mind inside its keep.

What galaxies to contemplate,
    so bring me texts and saturate!

Eighteen

Darkness cannot hold the hill
    that prismic light in boldness takes.

Night cannot suppress the joy
    the twilight's dancing hearth fire wakes.

He lifts his flagon to night's deep.
    He speaks his stories – red sparks fly!
    Stars wheel about his golden head
    as hours of sand-spun joy glide by.

A castled king –
    come dawn he roars.
    In one fell flash, the dark is done.

And everlasting cheer he strikes –
    as merry fire dances on.

Nineteen

In the self –
    all things.

In the self –
    wings.

Feeling the muse –
    height.

Feeling the void –
    night.

Journeying deep –
    peace.

Troubles to heart –
    cease.

Twenty

Steady, gentle
    are the hands
    that boldly bear these
    hidden bones –
    these rocking shores
    of foreign lands.

How vast the mind –
    sea meeting sea.
    How brave the eye
    unblind, the heart
    that moves the scalpel,
    opens me.

Twenty-One

I catch in hand, toad-like, this hour,
    and like a toad, it hops away.

I grasp the minutes, slipping, dewy.
    From my palm, takes flight the day.

The past – departed yet I see it,
    rich with detail, scrolling sly.

And future dreams, though non-existent
    cast their spells and charm my eye.

Where then dwell I? What, my country?
    Nothing I can comprehend.

So glide I through rough seas untroubled,
    watching time, my vessel bend.

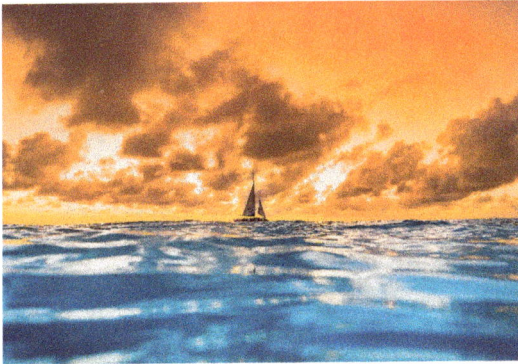

Twenty-Two

The journey long, the night air cold,
    will gates there be of pearl and gold?

If pearl –
    may end of journeys be
    upon the beach,
    beside the sea.

When lifetimes I have stayed, and more
    to sit, to rest upon the shore –
    what peace then shall descend on me,
    my gaze locked on the waving sea.

But let this not the last day be,
    nor let them fail – my company.
    For many journeys came before
    as I, creator, spun the lore
    of story souls who sought to be.

Let them, too, be –
    and merry, we
    by sunrise one another hold
    and weave new tales
    unthought
    untold.

Twenty-Three

The past, though a creature of pain –
    fear her not.

In mouth she holds grumblings and blame –
    fear her not.

To run from her names you her kill –
    fear her not.

Caught.
    Listen – insights she speaks.
    Fear her not.

Twenty-Four

From heights inside a dormant mind,
    all runs so clear, as mountain streams.

Might little doubt one's judgement – self.
    Might little seek a varied view.

Other minds are mountains, same,
    and unobstructed vistas wait

and drop the uniform approach,
    and there rise contemplations new.

Twenty-Five

I toil years and bear my tithe of yield
    for what?
    To tap the fleshy well of depths
    and find

the self unbounded, fathomless
    and free
    to bear the pleasure of unraveling
    the heart.

Naught else can compensate for this
    keen pain,
    but in the venturing to hear
    your voice.

Proclaim I then the joy of
    honeyed wealth,
    for feel I through the realms you waked
    to live.

Twenty-Six

A heart at work
    delivering its flight,
    gives not a pause
    for in to slip foul lies.

Heart brimming with
    strong wisdom taken in,
    drink, then drink!
    And flair the sail of skies.

Twenty-Seven

At lover's gaze night breaks – a sunrise.
　　Bleakest storms rage not pure dark.

For love, the lantern proudly carries,
　　flame aglow while page I mark.

Creating for sake of creating –
　　some tales knit sole by the will.

But carried on enchanted currents
　　stories penned rival the real.

Twenty-Eight

The aspen high speaks languages
    of silver and of water and of sun
    and teaches he the baby bird
    the melodies that lace his tongue.

So sit I in his company
    and listen to the stories told –
    how strong is wind
    how fleet is rain
    how summer's voice is pure as gold

– I think.

I bear not baby ears of birds
    nor ears electric of the bee
    but listen still, day after day must I
    that summer's chalice might I be.

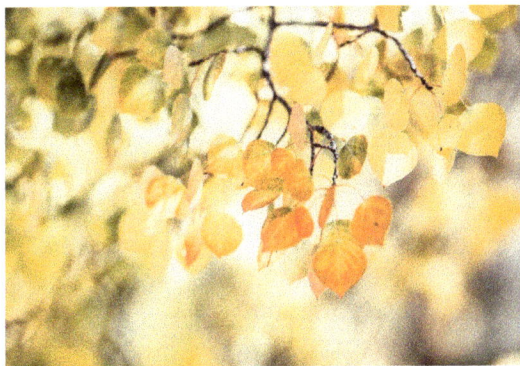

Twenty-Nine

Undisclosed, in silence speaks the heart
      and constant in his court hears words of love.

No friend truer counsel gives than heart,
      if heart is lightened, seasoned in its climb.

Heart, all strength,
      bears time
      bears fear
      bears pain.

Heart, dark engine, churns the night to day.
      Heart, with inner eye, sees ego's form
      and guides his bearer into peaceful climbs.

Thirty

Light from one great sun presents
one view.

And yet the earth it lights appears
unsound.

Where lay the landscapes certain in
my mind?

Instilled by visions, starlit yet
unmade?

Thirty-One

I am not one,
    I've lived not once,
    since I was born,
    such stars have wheeled.

In every hamlet
    where I've slept
    a piece of who
    I am sleeps still.

My figure person-like
    in glass,
    but by the memory
    truer known –

contorted form
    by all that's passed,
    each home has laid –
    joint, bone, joint, bone.

Thirty-Two

If thoughts, they echo –
    what are they?
    How far beyond
    a mind extend?

No fellow flesh-made
    traveler might
    deduce them true
    nor answers send.

Yet speaks the mind
    its silent way
    as if a greater
    mind to bend.

Waits one to catch
    these soundless words?

Such deepness none
    can comprehend.

Thirty-Three

Heart so quick to warn
    where last I fell.

Heart who first will hide
    before she looks.

Heart who keeps on film
    the moments pained.

Heart whose secrets keep
    in unshared books –

What might toughen little
    heart to bear
    the passing days as present
    time – as gifts.

Little eyes perceive
    abundant threats
    but little heart, be stout –
    a world to lift.

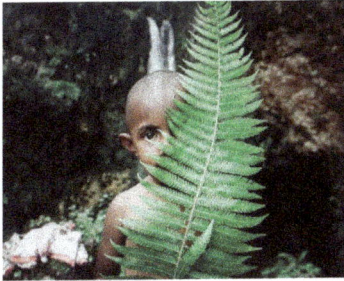

Thirty-Four

Today stands giant.
    I – a sprite,
    chin rubbing,
    fathoming
    this thundering.

Falter I,
    for fears resound –
    my shaken knees
    fold to the ground.

Then how shall I
    approach this fight?

But giant day
    kneels low to meet
    my eyes, to set
    me on my feet.

Fierce day stands not
    to sprites oppose.
    Instead
    he – teacher
    wisdom shows.

Thirty-Five

What antics when I turn my back
    do birds, does nature play?

To sit in stillness, holding watch
    is to unveil the day.

Thickets hide the eggy dreams
    of wrens who perfect seek
    to sew a nest, a softened stole
    where wrenlings soon shall sleep.

Across the lawn, the sparrows sweep
    each baby of the spring
    attending fast to masters teaching
    how to take to wing.

I steal away but when I must,
    when other duties call –
    for moments glimpsing nature's dance
    are precious most of all.

Thirty-Six

Acknowledge me
    from marrow's core – resounds the plea –
    then laud me more!

The ego head
    seeks rains of praise, on glory red
    its trim teeth graze.

With hungry eyes,
    tear wet and fixed, the ego lies
    for little kicks.

But street cred, fame,
    these are not wings – a coveted name –
    they're paper things.

The raging id
    shakes fist to sky when others won't
    reflect the lie

that it has weaved
    to turn their gaze on claims believed,
    on conjured craze.

What matters
    at the end of day, what flatters
    not, but hunger sates?

The words improved
    by day, by day; the belly soothed
    the workbench way.

Thirty-Seven

The ache of aloneness,
    abandonment, fear.
    The world once rushed bustling,
    silence – now here.

Aloneness, unrest are not
    chased by shed tears,
    and no friends intervene
    when oblivion leers.

The wisest of self must be
    stationed to steer
    into seas rich with challenge,
    where waves flash with cheer.

Thirty-Eight

A certain rapture manifests,
    eyes roving line to line of words,

when in a character – a glimpse
    of tendencies I know by heart.

A transport as to humble page
    I say – "it's me," and, reading on,

discover answers, blank before.
    So better made for life, I part.

Thirty-Nine

Cleave the body, sole to find
    no spirit – just a tide of blood.

Into earth plunge spade to find
    no seed-spun charm, but merest mud.

Rend the skull – there, no thoughts lie
    nor strains of music, reasons, laws.

Unfasten heartstrings deep within –
    just currents red, no valiant cause.

A rush of days though, hour to hour –
    problems knotted weave untangled,
    paintings beckoned, stories cast,
    the dawnlight splashed, the twilight spangled.

In this matter must reside
    a brilliant magic making djinn.
    And so I give to him my gaze –
    we move as one, a world to spin.

Forty

Forget not the misted midnight
    and its wolves
    for night wolves feast upon not bones
    but cares.
    Shun not that hour that miserable makes
    the anxious heart.
    Rather, the moment seize.

Like seasoned chops,
    on your doorstep starlit,
    lay out your angst.

Beckon nigh the fierce beasts
    And with them gnaw the grizzled meat.

Sit with your wolves in the still eye
    of aftercry –
    these loyals who night after night
    prove company.

Fear not your wolves
    for come tomorrow and dawn,
    the smile lighting you
    shall be truer
    wiser
    better friended.

Fully supped
    shall be your troubled heart.

Forty-One

Wild flowers cut and pressed
    and closed inside
    a book
    retain their faerie charms

fed not on light nor water
    rich with earth
    but dark
    and soaking in the leaves –

of paper –
    world of words.

Shine on, shine on
    sun shard
    illuminating valiant feats
    and stirring dashing hearts
    the brave embark
    and quest
    the truth to hunt, to win.

Forty-Two

I tried my hand at dry wine,
  but it hurried me to bed.
  A drop of scotch upon my lips
  encased my bones in led.

I swooned before the steeple's chime
  and knelt before the window stained.
  I shuddered at the altar's stair,
  but found no melody unchained.

So nothing brewed nor cobbled
  ever wakes the light I see –
  flickering live and winging,
  soaring o'er a beating sea.

It's in the berry summer moon
  and in stars bluing in the bleak.
  It's ferried on the river's waves
  and on the apple of your cheek.

The lift, the flight –
  pursued, it fails.
  But in the gold of racing dawn
  I feel its cold hand lift my chin.
  My fear of life, of death is gone.
  I've found a pathway, deeper in.

Forty-Three

'Tis nature tight to cling.

For do not oaken leaves grasp
    their winter white trees
    and iced ocean waves
    snatch frantically at the warm beach?

And do moon and sun
    and Earth not draw
    together with all space?

Yet toward letting go,
    in taking on full vertigo
    of deepest trek
    untold and unknown –

all nature slants.

Forty-Four

The secret to flight is to render
    an art out of pain.

Shun not the dark days,
    the teeth shined in wait,
    the gaze searching
    to seize
    and to damn.

The secret to flight, if you ask him,
    the bee will reveal
    is the gathering,
    grain by small grain
    of the day.

Lose not one shackle of ache.

The secret to flight is to cherish a turbulent mind
    and to bear marrowed bones
    and heart heavy −

by presence
    to shape into light.

Photography contributed by:

1. Jordon Connor
2. Sasha Freemind
3. Timothy Eberly
4. Evie S.
5. Steve Harvey
6. Jeremy Bishop
7. Beth Jnr
8. Edan Cohen
9. Klemen Vrankar
10. Marc Thunis
11. Luca Micheli
12. Matheus Ferrero
13. H. Heyerlein
14. Veit Hammer
15. Grace Evans
16. Artem Sapegin
17. Benjamin Davies
18. Hayden Scott
19. Valdemaras D.
20. Marianna Smiley
21. Edrick Krozndijk
22. Alexey Malakhov
23. Erik Kerits
24. Simon Fitall
25. Aziz Acharki
26. James Bekkers
27. Chilherme Stecanella
28. Katie Moum
29. Jose Mizrahi
30. Sergey Pesterev
31. Fidel Fernando
32. Robin Benad
33. Asso Myron
34. Ben Curry
35. Kev Kindred
36. Roseanna Smith
37. Mauro Gigli
38. Aaron Burden
39. Dollar Gill

Free eBook

Night Swiftly Falling
by Tricia D. Wagner

Eight-year-old Swift is lost in dreams of sea legends and pirate adventures, until an encounter with the deadly power of the ocean shocks him into reality. Swift struggles to hang onto his childhood fantasies, but his new understanding of the fragile nature of life and friendships threatens to swamp his hope. Under the guidance of his older brother, Caius, Swift must learn to brave the challenging waves of change without losing himself to their destruction.

Also by Tricia D. Wagner

SWIFT & THE STAR OF ATLANTIS SERIES

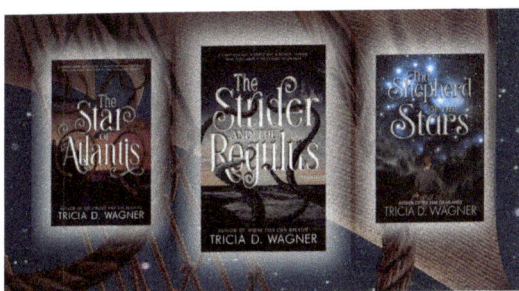

A STARRY-EYED BOY. A CRYPTIC MAP. A MYTHICAL TREASURE. WHAT PERILS AWAIT IN THE CHASING OF DREAMS?

AS SWIFT LIVES UP TO HIS NAME AND HIS FAMILY LEGACY, YOUNG ADULTS RECEIVE A FAST-PACED FANTASY THAT WILL APPEAL NOT JUST ON THE ADVENTURE OR FANTASY LEVELS, BUT IN MATTERS OF THE HEART AS THE YOUNG STRUGGLE FOR INDEPENDENCE AND ACTION IN THE FACE OF PARENTAL RESTRICTIONS. TRICIA D. WAGNER'S ATTENTION TO PAIRING PSYCHOLOGICAL STRUGGLE WITH THE ADVENTURE OF FINDING A PROMISED TREASURE CREATES A STORY THAT PULLS ON THE EMOTIONS OF YOUNG READERS AS IT SATISFIES THEIR DESIRE FOR ACTION AND ADVENTURE.

-D. Donovan, Senior Reviewer, Midwest Book Review

Also by Tricia D. Wagner

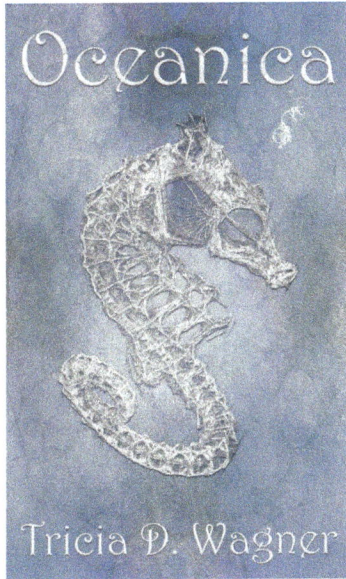

OCEANICA

IN *OCEANICA*, TRICIA D. WAGNER CELEBRATES OUR SEAS AND OCEANS, OUR DASHING WATER WORLDS. SHE CAPTURES THE JOY, THE REVELING IN THE JOURNEY OF CHASING THE PRESENT. AND THROUGHOUT THESE THIRTY POEMS, SHE HIGHLIGHTS HOW SPECIAL CAN BE OUR CONNECTION WITH NATURE, ESPECIALLY OUR COASTS, SEAS, OUR OCEANS. FOR THESE LEND HER POWER AND INSPIRATION FOR CREATIVE WRITING.

Also by Tricia D. Wagner

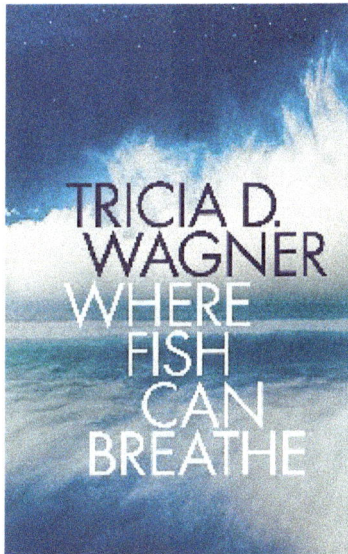

WHERE FISH CAN BREATHE

TEN-YEAR-OLD SWIFT LONGS TO BE AS GROWN UP AS HIS BROTHERS, BUT CONFRONTING HIMSELF IN THE WILDS OF THE NORTH ATLANTIC, HE MUST CONTEND WITH WHAT IT MEANS TO BE A MAN.

Also by Tricia D. Wagner

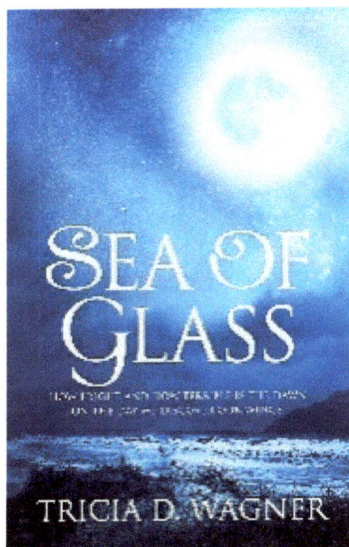

Sea of Glass

When an old angler presses Teo to seek a goddess—the Sea Angel—for rescue, Teo sets out along Baja's wild coast to test whether help can be found at the hands of the gods.

To learn the truth, he must look beyond legends and summon the courage to challenge his papá.

And to reach freedom, he must tap his own strength, hidden beneath wounds laid by glass.

Also by Tricia D. Wagner

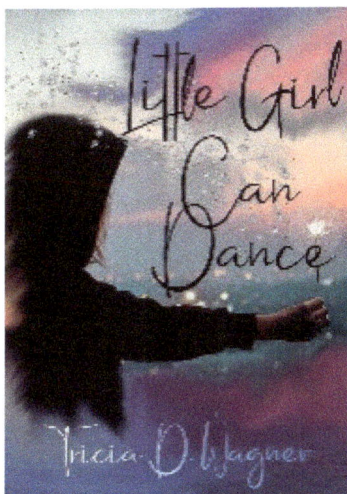

LITTLE GIRL CAN DANCE

A DANCER. A CREATURE. A SPIRE-CAPPED AND LONELY BOARDING SCHOOL.

LITTLE GIRL CAN DANCE IS A SPELLBINDING TALE TOLD OVER SIX SWEEPING ACTS. TRICIA D. WAGNER'S SIGNATURE STYLE IS ON TOP FORM IN THIS BEAUTIFUL NOVELLA.

A WONDERFUL FUSION OF POETIC PROSE AND LIMITLESS IMAGINATION PLUNGES YOU STRAIGHT INTO ANDROMEDA'S MESMERISING WORLD.

PREPARE TO HAVE YOUR HEART BROKEN AND MENDED AGAIN IN THIS SHORT BUT STUNNING FABLE.

*-**ELEANOR HAWKEN**, AUTHOR OF THE BLUE LADY AND SAMMY FERAL'S DIARIES OF WEIRD*

About the Author

TRICIA D. WAGNER IS AN AWARD-WINNING NOVELIST, POET, AND SHORT STORY WRITER. SHE GREW UP IN AMARILLO, TEXAS, CHASING STORMS, RIDING STALLIONS, SOJOURNING THROUGH PAINTED CANYONS, DISAPPEARING INTO FLOATING MESAS UNDER STARRY SKIES.

SHE NOW LIVES IN ROCKFORD, ILLINOIS (THOUGH THE TRUTH IS, SHE'S A CITIZEN OF A DOZEN FICTIONAL COUNTRIES.) TRICIA WORKS IN EDUCATION AND LIVES DAY TO DAY WONDERSTRUCK BUT LUCKILY CAN FEEL HER WAY ABOUT THIS TERRIFYING, BEAUTIFUL EARTH THROUGH WRITING.

TRICIA HAS PIECES PUBLISHED IN THE *WRITE CITY MAGAZINE*, *CHICAGO NEWA*, *WORD OF ART 3D*, *LITERARY YARD*, AND *MIDWEST REVIEW*.

Author's Note

I love connecting with readers and writers. If, you're interested in stories, then you're a kindred spirit to me, and I have lots more in store for you.

To quote another kindred spirit in writing, Jedi Master Stephen King:

"Writing is magic, as much as the water of life as any other art. The water is free. So drink. Drink and be filled up."

If you're interested not only in stories, but in story creation, visit my website and sign up to receive a FREE **Story Kickoff Character Worksheet.**

I designed this tool for that first moment of getting our feet wet at the brink of a story.

To get your FREE worksheet, visit:
www.TriciaWagner.com